Cards with Vellum

Mieke van den Akker

FORTE PUBLISHERS

Contents

Second printing April 2004
ISBN 90 5877 368 x

This is a publication from
Forte Publishers BV
P.O. Box 1394
3500 BJ Utrecht
The Netherlands

For more information about the creative books available from Forte Uitgevers:
www.hobby-party.com

Publisher: Els Neele
Editor: Hilde Vinken
Final editing: Gina Kors-Lambers
Photography and digital image editing:
Piet Pulles Fotografie, Waalwijk,
the Netherlands
Faerie Poppets pictures (copyright Christine Haworth) used with the permission of Jalekro bv.
Cover and inner design:
BADE creatieve communicatie, Baarn,
the Netherlands
Translation: TextCase, Groningen,
the Netherlands

Preface

When we had the satin finish cards in our hands, we were completely sold. It has a lovely, classic appearance and when combined with various types of vellum, it is truly radiant. You can use it to make wedding cards, anniversary cards, birth cards, in short, you can use it for any type of celebration. The great thing is that the five colours are also available as paper, which is excellent to use for punching. Matching satin finish envelopes are the perfect finishing touch. Once you have made your first card, you will not believe that you have made it yourself.

Have fun making the vellum cards.

Mieke van den Akker   Loes Hildering

Techniques

A special technique is required if you wish to punch using square punches. Hold the punch upside down so that you can see what you are doing. You will then be able to punch a continuous line. Punch the second time with the punch overlapping the first punch mark by 1 mm, the third time with the punch overlapping the second mark punch by 1 mm, etc. A frame punch with lines on the inside is used differently. For the second punch, place the punch over the line already punched. It will fit exactly. Practice on a piece of scrap paper before making a card. Paper or vellum is usually used for punching. Make sure you shake the punch well each time, because very small pieces of paper may sometimes be stuck in it.

A strip of card is cut off of many of these cards and then stuck back on later (to make the card complete). Vellum which is punched with a art punch is stuck between the front of the card and the strip which has been cut off using double-sided adhesive tape to make an attractive pattern in the card. Stick mica in front of it to give it strength. The card will then be transparent. It looks really nice if you decorate the edges of the card with border stickers. Instead of vellum, you could also use satin finish paper which is the same colour as the card. It is used in the same way as the vellum. Punched daisies are placed on the soft, red mat and pressed down or turned in the middle using a large embossing stylus to raise them up. Fold the punched leaves double and place them at an angle in a Ridge Master. Fold them open to give you attractive leaves.

The transparent stickers are excellent to use. You can, for example, stick them on vellum regardless of whether it has been punched with a art punch or not. They look particularly good on the mini collage cards.

1. The materials used in this book.

2. The most attractive cards are made using a combination of vellum, 3D cutting sheets and punches.

3. Transparent stickers and border stickers really suit these cards.

4. Satin finish cards in five different colours and three different types make everything complete.

Materials

- ❏ Photo glue
- ❏ Silicon glue
- ❏ Double-sided adhesive tape
- ❏ Foam tape
- ❏ Ridge Master
- ❏ Embossing tray
- ❏ Embossing stylus (large and small)
- ❏ Cutting machine
- ❏ Pair of scissors
- ❏ Soft, red mat

Daisies

Card 1

Satin finish card: blue square
• Satin finish paper: blue
(12.5 x 12.5 cm) • Vellum:
blue/green • Punch pattern 1 •
Bite punch • Figure punch: daisies
• Medium punch: daisy and beech leaf
• Art punch: flower • Stickers: gold (1016 and 3101)

Make a copy of the punch pattern (see page 10).
Cut it out slightly bigger and use a small amount
of photo glue to stick a piece of vellum to the
back of it. Turn the punch over and carefully
punch all the squares. Cut along the outside line.
Remove the copy of the pattern from the vellum.
Use the bite punch to punch the corners of the
vellum. Stick the vellum on the card and stick a
square transparent sticker in the middle. Punch
three large daisies and three beech leaves out of
the paper and three small daisies out of the vellum. Use the red mat and the large embossing
stylus to press and turn in the middle of the
daisies to raise them up. Use silicon glue to first
stick the three large daisies on the transparent
square. Next, stick the small daisies on the large
daisies and, finally, stick pearls on them. Fold the
three leaves double and put them at an angle in
the Ridge Master. Fold them open and use silicon
glue to stick them under the flowers. Stick a

border sticker around the edges of the vellum.
Stick gold circles from the square transparent
stickers in the middle of the patterns.

Card 2

Satin finish card: blue • Satin finish paper: blue
(12.5 x 12.5 cm) • Vellum: blue/green • Figure punch:
balloon • Medium punch: beech leaf • Stickers: gold
(226, 1016 and 3101)

Cut a strip from the vellum (5.5 x 15 cm) and use
photo glue to stick it on the card. Stick border
stickers along the sides of the vellum. Stick two
transparent squares on the vellum. Punch twelve
balloons and six beech leaves out of the satin
finish paper and six small balloons out of the vellum. Fold the beech leaves double and put them
at an angle in a Ridge Master. Place a large drop
of silicon glue in the middle of one of the transparent squares. Use a pair of scissors to puff up the
paper balloons. Place three of the paper balloons
slightly overlapping each other in a circle on the
drop of glue. Place the three vellum balloons
inside the paper balloons and place three pearls
in the middle. Finally, use silicon glue to stick the
three ridged leaves under the flower you have
just made. Repeat this on the second transparent
square. Place gold circles in the corners of the
card. Stick a text sticker at the top of the card.

Card 3

Satin finish card: blue • Satin finish paper: blue (12.5 x 12.5 cm) • Vellum: blue/green • Figure punch: daisy • Art punch: flower • Embossing stencil AE 1202 • Stickers: gold (841)

Cut a 7.5 cm wide strip off of the front of the card. Use the stencil to emboss both parts of the front of the card. Cut a strip from the vellum (5 x 15 cm). Turn the art punch over and punch five continuous patterns. Stick double-sided adhesive tape along the edge of the strip to stick it on the card. Take the embossed strip of card and stick it on the vellum. Cut it so that it is level with the back of the card. The card is now complete again. Punch five daisies out of the paper. Use the embossing stylus and the soft mat to puff them up. Stick them on the patterns. Stick a pearl in the middle of the daisies. Stick a border sticker along the punched edges.

Card 4

Satin finish card: blue square • Satin finish paper: blue (12.5 x 12.5 cm) • Vellum: blue/green • Art punch: autumn • Figure punch: daisy • Medium punch: daisy and beech leaf • Stickers: gold (1016 and 3101)

Cut an 8 cm wide strip off of the front of the card. Use the frame punch to punch a continuous pattern along the edge. Use double-sided adhesive tape to make the card complete with the vellum. Stick a transparent sticker in the middle of the vellum standing on a point. Punch three large daisies and three beech leaves out of the paper. Punch three small daisies out of the vellum. Using the red mat and the large embossing stylus, rotate the stylus in the centre of the daisies to raise the leaves. First, use silicon glue to stick the three large daisies on the square sticker. Next, stick the small daisies and pearls on top. Fold the leaves double and place them at an angle in a Ridge Master and then fold them open. Slide these leaves under the daisies. Stick a border sticker along the punched border and gold circles in the middle of the edges of the punched patterns.

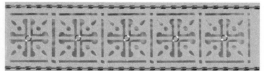

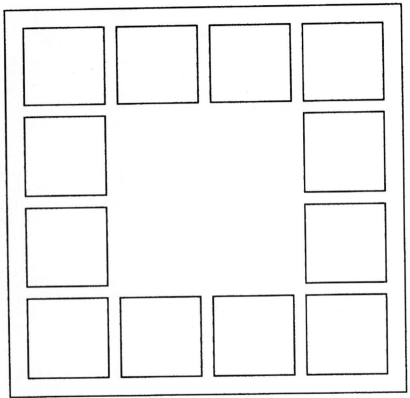

Punch pattern 1

Elves

Card 1

Satin finish card: pink square • Cutting sheet:
Faerie Poppets (99081/3 and 99011/13) • Mica: A4
• Figure punch: daisy • Art punch: flower • Stickers:
gold (3103 and 1016)

Cut a 4.5 cm wide strip off of the front of the
card. Cut a strip from the background paper
(5 x 12.5 cm) and punch the art punch pattern
five times in this strip. Use double-sided adhesive
tape to stick the strip on the front of the card.
Make the card complete by sticking the other
strip on the background paper and cutting it
level with the back of the card. Stick a border
sticker along the edges of the punched border.
Stick an oval sticker on the background paper,
cut it out and stick a picture on it. Punch seven
daisies and use the soft mat and the embossing
stylus to puff them up. Then stick them on the
punched border. Decorate the card with circles.

Card 2

Satin finish card: pink • Satin finish paper: pink
• Cutting sheet: Faerie Poppets (99011/13)

• Mica: A4 • Art punch: square • Figure punch: daisy
• Stickers: gold (1016 and 3103)

Cut a 4.5 cm wide strip off of the front of the card.
Cut a strip from the paper (5 x 15 cm) and punch
six continuous patterns in it. Use double-sided
adhesive tape to stick this strip on the front of the
card. Make the card complete with the other strip
of card and cut it level with the back of the card.
Stick a border sticker along the edges. Stick an
oval sticker on the paper, cut it out and stick a
picture on it. Punch six daisies out of the paper.
Use the mat and the embossing stylus to puff
them up and stick them on the punched patterns.
Stick a gold dot in the middle of each daisy.

Card 3

Satin finish card: pink • Satin finish paper: pink
(12.5 x 12.5 cm) • Vellum: Faerie Poppets (99082/3)
• Mica: A4 • Figure punch: daisy • Embossing stencil:
AE 1203 • Stickers: gold (1016)

Emboss a 7 cm wide strip on the left-hand side of
the front of the card and make a curved line. Cut

the card off along this line. Make the card complete with mica and double-sided adhesive tape. Use
double-sided adhesive tape to stick a piece of vellum against the back of the mica. Punch three daisies out of the paper and stick them on the card.
Stick a border sticker along the edge of the mica.

Card 4

*Satin finish card: pink mini collage • Vellum: Faerie
Poppets (99082/3) • Cutting sheet: Faerie Poppets*

(99081/3) • *Stickers: gold (226 and 3101)*
Stick four transparent squares on the background paper and cut them out. Use foam tape
to stick the squares on the card. Stick a square
on the vellum, cut it out and stick it on a passepartout frame. Stick another transparent square
on the back of the passepartout frame. Cut the
picture out, stick it on the card and make it 3D.
Add a text sticker.

Marriage

Card 1

*Satin finish card: green square • Vellum: forget-me-
nots • Cutting sheet: Nel van Veen (2228) • Mica:
A4 • Art punch: flower • Figure punch: daisy •
Stickers: gold (1016 and 3101)*
Cut the card diagonally 2 cm from the corners.
Cut a strip from the vellum (5 x 15 cm) and punch
four continuous patterns in it. Use double-sided
adhesive tape to stick this strip on the card. Also
stick the other strip back on the card to make the
card complete. Stick a triangular piece of vellum

in the top right-hand corner and the bottom left-
hand corner. Stick the transparent sticker on the
vellum and cut it out. Use foam tape to stick it on
the card. Punch four daisies out of the vellum
and stick them on the punched border. Cut the
picture out, stick it on the card and make it 3D.
Decorate the card with border stickers.

Card 2

*Satin finish card: green • Satin finish paper: green
• Vellum: forget-me-nots • Cutting sheet: Nel van
Veen (2228) • Embossing stencil: EH 1804 •
Stickers: gold (3101)*
Cut a 1.5 cm strip off of the front of the card.
Emboss the edge and cut it decoratively. Stick a

round sticker on the paper and cut it out. Use foam tape to stick it on the card. Cut the picture out, stick it on the card and make it 3D.

Card 3

Satin finish card: green • Satin finish paper: green • Vellum: forget-me-nots • Cutting sheet: Nel van Veen (2228) • Embossing stencil: EH 1804 • Stickers: gold (3101)

Cut a 1.5 cm wide strip off of the front of the card. Emboss the edge and cut it decoratively. Make the card complete with the vellum. Stick three transparent squares on the paper and cut them out. Use foam tape to stick them on the

card. Cut the pictures out, stick them on the card and make them 3D.

Card 4

Satin finish card: green mini collage • Satin finish paper: green • Vellum: forget-me-nots • Cutting sheet: Nel van Veen (2228) • Stickers: gold (3101)

Stick four squares on the paper and one square on the vellum. Use foam tape to stick the four squares on the card. Cut the pictures out, stick them on the squares and make them 3D. Stick the vellum on the passepartout frame and then stick a transparent square against the back. Stick some gold circles on the squares.

Tulips

Card 1

Satin finish card: white mini collage • Satin finish paper: white • Vellum: tulips (Pergamano) • Art punch: square • Figure punch: daisy • Medium punch: daisy • Stickers: gold (3101) • Adhesive stones: blue

Punch five patterns out of the vellum with space in between them. Stick transparent squares on

them and cut them out. Stick one square on the passepartout frame and stick a transparent square on it. Use foam tape to stick the other four patterns on the card. Punch three large daisies and three small daisies out of the vellum. Punch three daisies out of the satin finish paper and use the soft mat and the embossing stylus to puff them up. First, stick the large and small daisies on top of each other. Stick small circles in the middle of the flowers. Stick adhesive stones in the middle of the patterns.

1.

2.

3.

4.

Card 2

Satin finish card: white square • Satin finish paper: white • Shiny vellum: green • Vellum: tulips (Pergamano) • Punch pattern 2 • Figure punch: daisy • Medium punch: daisy and beech leaf

Make a copy of punch pattern 2 (see page 30). Cut the pattern out slightly bigger and use a small amount of photo glue to stick a piece of vellum to the back. Punch twelve continuous patterns as shown in the photograph. This must be done very accurately. Carefully cut around the outer edge. Remove the copy of the pattern and stick the vellum on the card. Punch three large daisies out of the paper. Punch three daisies out of the vellum. Use the soft mat and the embossing stylus to puff them up and stick them on top of each other. Punch three leaves out of the green vellum. Fold the leaves and put them at an angle in a Ridge Master. Open the leaves and stick them under the flowers. Stick pearls in the middle of the flowers. Stick silver circles on the patterns.

Card 3

Satin finish card: white square • Vellum: tulips (Pergamano) • Stickers: gold (822 and 1016) • Organza ribbon: white

Cut a strip from the vellum (12.5 x 13.5 cm) and make sure the tulips are facing the right way.

Punch four continuous patterns along one side. Fold the vellum around the card and use double-sided adhesive tape to stick it to the back of the card. Stick two butterflies on the vellum and cut them out. Bend the wings and stick the butterflies in the middle of the card. Stick border stickers around the patterns and around the edge of the card. Tie the ribbon around the card.

Card 4

Satin finish card: white squareo Satin finish paper: white • Vellum: tulips (Pergamano) • Figure punch: daisy • Medium punch: daisy • Art punch: square • Stickers: gold (1016 and 3101)

Cut a 6 cm wide strip off of the front of the card. Make the card complete with the vellum. Punch two patterns, three small and three large daisies out of the vellum. Punch three small daisies out of the white paper. Cut the patterns out and use foam tape to stick them on the card standing on their points. Puff the daisies up and stick them on top of each other. Stick some gold stickers and a border sticker on the card.

Congratulations

Card 1

Satin finish card: white square • Vellum: silver text (Pergamano) • Mica: A4 • Stickers: silver (822, 841, 1016 and 3102) • Organza ribbon: white

Cut the front of the card diagonally through the middle. Make the card complete with the mica. Stick vellum behind it. Stick border stickers · around the edges of the mica. Stick the round sticker and the butterflies on the vellum and cut them out. Use foam tape to stick the circle on the card. Bend the wings of the butterflies using a pair of scissors. Apply glue to the middle of the butterflies and stick them on the card. Finally, tie the ribbon around the card.

Card 2

Satin finish card: white square • Satin finish paper: white • Vellum: silver text (Pergamano) • Mica: A4 • Figure punch: daisy • Medium punch: daisy and beech leaf • Embossing stencil: AE 1203 • Stickers: silver (1016 and 3102)

Emboss the front of the card. Cut an 8 cm wide strip off of the front of the card. Use double-sided adhesive tape to make the card complete with the mica. Stick vellum behind it. Cut a 3 cm wide strip from the strip you cut off of the card and use double-sided adhesive tape to stick it in the middle of the mica. Stick border stickers

along the edges. Stick a round transparent sticker on the vellum and cut it out. Use foam tape to stick it on the card. Punch three large daisies and three small daisies out of the paper Use the soft mat and the embossing stylus to puff them up. Stick them on top of each other and stick a pearl on them. Punch three leaves

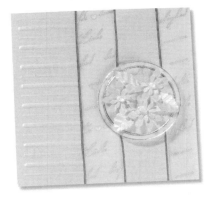

and fold them double. Place them at an angle in a Ridge Master. Fold them open and stick them under the flowers.

Card 3

Satin finish card: white square • Satin finish paper: white • Vellum: gold text (Pergamano) • Mica: A4 • Figure punch: daisy • Medium punch: daisy and beech leaf • *Embossing stencil: AE 1203 • Stickers: gold (3103)*

Cut a 5 cm wide strip off of the front of the card. Emboss lines on the front of the card. Emboss a decorative line and cut the card off along the line. Use double-sided adhesive tape to make the card complete with the mica. Stick vellum behind the mica. Punch three small daisies and three large daisies out of the paper. Use the soft mat and the embossing stylus to puff them up. Stick the oval sticker on the vellum and cut it out. Use foam tape to stick it on the card. Stick the flowers on top of each other and stick three pearls in the middle of each flower. Punch three leaves out of the paper and fold them double. Place them at an angle in a Ridge Master. Fold them open and stick them under the flowers.

Card 4

Satin finish card: white mini collage • Satin finish paper: white • Vellum: music • Figure punch: daisy • Medium punch: daisy and beech leaf • Stickers: silver (1016 and 3101)

Cut the front of the card diagonally through the middle. Make the card complete with the vellum. Stick a transparent square on the vellum and cut it out. Use foam tape to stick it in the middle of the card. Punch a large daisy, a small daisy and three beech leaves out of the paper. Punch a daisy out of the vellum. Puff the daisies up and stick them on top of each other on the card. Fold the beech leaves double and put them at an angle in a Ridge Master. Fold them open and stick them under the flower. Stick border stickers on the lines and around the edges. Stick some silver circles on the card.

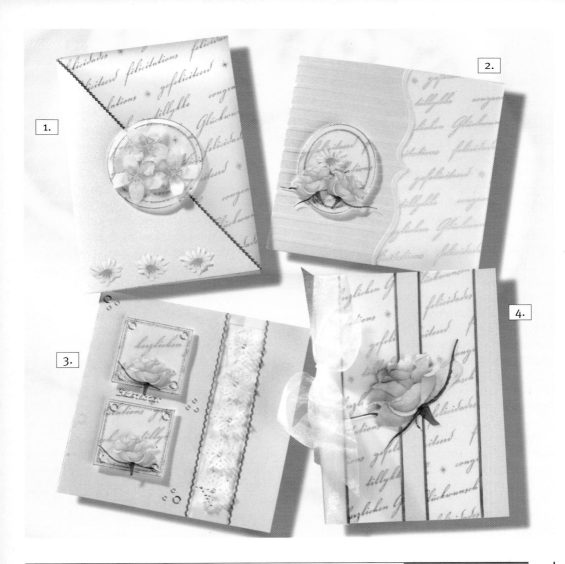

Romantic

Card 1 (on the cover)

Satin finish card: white • Vellum: gold text (Pergamano) • Cutting sheet: green/white flowers (Marjolein) • Stickers: gold (1016 and 3101)

Cut the front of the card diagonally through the middle. Use double-sided adhesive tape to make the card complete with the vellum. Stick a border sticker along the diagonal line. Stick a round sticker on the vellum and cut it out. Use double-sided adhesive tape to stick it in the middle of the card. Stick some flowers on the circle and at the bottom of the card.

Card 2 (on the cover)

Satin finish card: white square • Vellum: gold text (Pergamano) • Cutting sheet: green/white flowers (Marjolein) • Mica: thick, A4 • Embossing stencil: AE 1203 • Stickers: gold (3103)

Cut a 5 cm wide strip off of the front of the card. Emboss lines on the front of the card. Emboss a decorative border and carefully cut the card off along this line. Use double-sided adhesive tape to make the card complete with the mica. Use double-sided adhesive tape to stick vellum behind the mica. Stick the oval sticker on the vellum and cut it out. Use foam tape to stick it on the card. Use silicon glue to stick some flowers on the oval.

Card 3

Satin finish card: white • Satin finish paper: white • Vellum: gold text (Pergamano) • Cutting sheet: green/white flowers (Marjolein) • Art punch: square • Stickers: gold (1016 and 3101)

Cut a 5 cm wide strip off of the front of the card. Use double-sided adhesive tape to make the card complete with the mica. Stick a 2.5 cm wide strip of white card on the front of the card. Cut a strip from the paper (5 x 12.5 cm) and punch five continuous patterns in it. Use double-sided adhesive tape to stick it behind the mica. Punch five patterns out of the vellum and cut them out separately. Puff them up and stick them on the mica. Stick two squares on the vellum and cut them out. Use foam tape to stick them on the card. Stick some flowers on the squares. Decorate the card with some stickers.

Card 4

Satin finish card: white • Vellum: gold text (Pergamano) • Cutting sheet: green/white flowers (Marjolein) • Stickers: gold (1016) • Organza ribbon: white

Cut two strips from the vellum (3 x 15 cm) and use photo glue to stick them on the card. Stick border stickers along the edges. Stick a flower on the card. Tie a ribbon around the card.

Dreams

Card 1

Satin finish card: green square • Cutting sheet: Faerie Poppets snail (99081/5 and 99081/3) • Stickers: gold (1016 and 3101) • Art punch: square

Cut a strip from the background paper (5 x 12.5 cm) and punch five continuous patterns in it. Stick this strip on the right-hand side of the card. Stick a transparent sticker on the background paper and cut it out. Use foam tape to stick it on the card. Cut out the picture and stick it on the card. Decorate the card with stickers.

Card 2

Satin finish card: green square • Cutting sheet: Faerie Poppets (99081/3) • Bite punch • Embossing stencil: AE 12 • Stickers: gold (3103)

Cut an 8 cm wide strip off of the front of the card. Emboss the front, make a border and cut the edge decoratively. Use double-sided adhesive tape to make the card complete with the background paper. Use the bite punch to punch the corners. Stick the sticker on the background paper and cut it out. Cut the picture out, stick it on the card and make it 3D.

Card 3

Satin finish card: green square • Cutting sheets: Faerie Poppets (99081/3) and Nel van Veen (2228) • Art punch: square • Stickers: gold (1016 and 3101)

Cut a 5 cm wide strip off of the front of the card. Cut a strip from the background paper (5 x 12.5 cm) and punch five continuous patterns in it. Use double-sided adhesive tape to stick this strip on the card. Make the card complete with the strip you cut off. Stick border stickers along the edges. Stick two squares on the background paper and cut them out. Use foam tape to stick them on the card. Cut the pictures out, stick them on the squares and make them 3D.

Roses

Card 1

Satin finish card: pink mini collage • Satin finish paper: pink • Cutting sheet: pink roses (Marjolein) • Figure punch: daisy • Medium punch: daisy • Stickers: gold (3101)

Stick four transparent squares on four rose pictures. Cut them out and use foam tape to stick them in the corners of the card. Punch five small daisies and a large daisy. Stick four small daisies in the middle of the outer sections of the card. Stick a transparent square on the passepartout frame. Stick two punched flowers on it and stick a transparent square on top so that the flowers are in between. Decorate the card with gold circles.

Card 2

Satin finish card: pink square • Satin finish paper: pink (12.5 x 2.5 cm) • Cutting sheet: pink roses (Marjolein) • Art punch: square • Figure punch: daisy • Embossing stencil: AE 1203 • Stickers: gold (1016 and 3101)

Emboss the front of the card. Cut an 8 cm wide strip off of the front of the card. Cut a strip from the paper (5 x 12.5 cm). Punch five continuous patterns in the strip and use double-sided adhesive tape to stick it on the card. Make the card complete with the strip you cut off. Stick border stickers along the edges. Stick two transparent squares on two rose pictures and cut them out. Use foam tape to stick them on the card. Punch five daisies, puff them up and stick them on the patterns. Stick a pearl in the middle of the daisies.

Card 3

Satin finish card: pink mini collage • Background paper: roses and dots (Marjolein) • Cutting sheet: pink roses (Marjolein) • Stickers: gold (822)

Stick two transparent squares on one background sheet and two on the other background sheet. Cut them out and use foam tape to stick them in the corners of the card. Stick three butterflies on a background sheet and cut them out. Fold them double and use a pair of scissors to bend the wings. Apply glue to the middle of the butterflies and stick them in the empty sections. Stick a picture of a rose behind the passepartout frame. Stick a text sticker on the card.

Card 4

Satin finish card: pink mini collage • Satin finish paper: white • Cutting sheet: pink roses (Marjolein) • Stickers: gold (1016) • Text sticker • Organza ribbon

Stick border stickers on the lines of the card and stick a couple of gold circles on the card. Cut the rose out, stick it in the bottom left-hand corner of the card and make it 3D. Cut a strip from white satin finish paper (6 x 6 cm) and stick it behind the passepartout frame. Stick a text sticker in the middle. Tie the ribbon around the card and use silicon glue to stick it to the back of the card.

Summer bouquet

Card 1

Satin finish card: green mini collage • Satin finish paper: green (12.5 x 12.5 cm) • Cutting sheet: green/white flowers (Marjolein) • Art punch: flower • Figure punch: daisy • Stickers: gold (3101)

Punch four patterns out of the paper and stick square transparent stickers on top. Cut them out and use foam tape to stick them in the corners of the card. Cut a flower out of the cutting sheet and stick it on the transparent sticker. Stick this on the passepartout frame. Stick another sticker on top so that the flowers are between the stickers. Punch four daisies out of the paper. Use the red mat and the embossing stylus to puff them up. Stick them on the patterns. Decorate the card with circles.

Card 2

Satin finish card: green square • Vellum: lilies • Cutting sheet: IT 353 (Marianne Design) • Art punch: windmill • Figure punch: daisy • Embossing stencil: AE 1201 • Stickers: gold (3103)

Cut a 9 cm wide strip off of the front of the card. Emboss the front of the card and the strip. Cut a strip from the vellum (5 x 12.5 cm) and use the art punch to punch five continuous patterns in it. Use double-sided adhesive tape to stick this strip on the card. Make the card complete using the strip you cut off. Stick the oval on the vellum and cut it out. Use double-sided adhesive tape to stick it on the card. Cut out the picture and stick it on the oval. Punch five daisies out of the vellum. Puff them up and stick them on the patterns. Decorate the card with gold circles.

Card 3

Satin finish card: green • Vellum: clover (Pergamano) • Cutting sheet: green/white flowers (Marjolein) • Mica: A4 • Embossing stencil: AE 1201 • Stickers: gold (1016 and 3101)

Cut a 5.5 cm wide strip off of the front of the card. Use double-sided adhesive tape to make the card complete with the mica. Stick vellum behind the mica. Stick border stickers along the edges. Stick three transparent squares on three flowers. Cut them out and

use foam tape to stick them on the card.
Decorate the card with circles.

Card 4

*Satin finish card: green mini collage • Satin finish
paper: green, A4 • Cutting sheet: green/white flowers
(Marjolein) • Stickers: gold (3101)*
Cut four flowers slightly bigger out of the cutting sheet. Stick them on the A4 sheet and
carefully cut them out. Use foam tape to stick
them in the corners of the card. Carefully cut
out another flower and stick it on a transparent
square. Stick it on the passepartout frame and
stick a transparent square on top. Decorate the
card with gold circles.

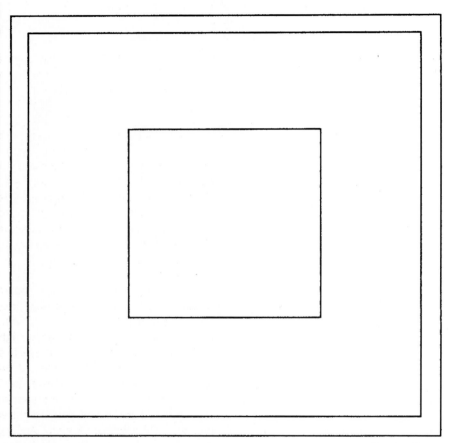

Punch pattern 2

Butterflies and roses

Card (preface, left)

Satin finish card: white • Vellum: Faerie Poppets (99082/4) • Mica: A4 • Stickers: butterfly (822 and 843) and gold (3101)

Cut a 5 cm wide strip off of the front of the card. Make the card complete with the mica. Use double-sided adhesive tape to stick the vellum behind the mica. Stick border stickers around the mica. Stick two transparent squares on the vellum with the small flowers. Cut the squares out. Use foam tape to stick them on the card standing on their points. Stick two butterflies on the vellum and cut them out. Use a pair of scissors to bend the wings, and stick them on the card.

Card (preface, right)

Satin finish card: white square • Vellum: Faerie Poppets (99082/4) • Figure punch: daisy • Art punch: Milky Way • Stickers: gold (3101, 822 and 1016)

Cut a 5.5 cm wide strip off of the front of the card. Cut a strip from the vellum (12.5 x 5 cm). Punch four continuous patterns in the strip. Use double-sided adhesive tape to stick this strip on the card. Make the card complete with the strip you cut off. Punch four daisies out of the vellum and use the red mat and the embossing stencil to puff them up. Stick them in the middle of the punched patterns. Stick a pearl in the middle of the daisies. Stick two squares and a butterfly on the vellum and cut them out. Use foam tape to stick the squares on the card. Bend the wings of the butterfly, and stick it on the card.

Card 1

Satin finish card: white • Vellum: roses (Pergamano) • Mica: A4 • Stickers: gold (1016 and 3101)

Stick three squares on the vellum and cut them out. Cut the front of the card through the middle. Make the card complete with the mica. Stick the vellum behind the mica. Use foam tape to stick the squares on the card. Decorate the card with border stickers.

Card 2

Satin finish card: white square • Vellum: Faerie Poppets (99082/3) • Stickers: gold (822, 1016 and 3102)

Cut a strip from the vellum (12.5 x 14 cm). Cut the vellum so that the pictures are on the right-hand side. Use double-sided adhesive tape to stick it to the back of the card next to the fold. Stick the round transparent sticker and two butterflies on the vellum and cut them out. Use foam tape to stick the circle on the card. Fold the butterflies double and fold them open again. Apply glue to the middle of the butterflies and stick them on the card. Stick a gold border sticker or text sticker next to the pictures.

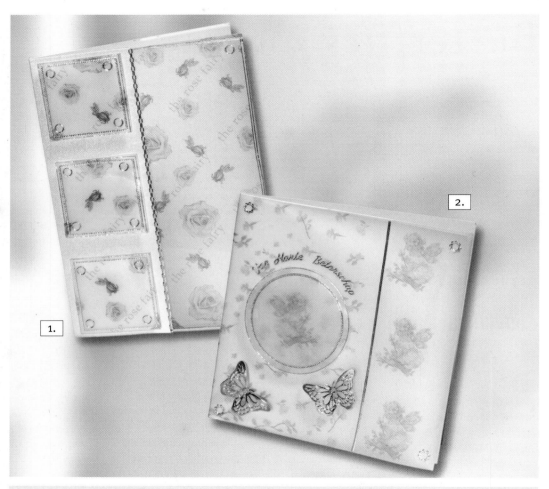

1.

2.

Many thanks to Romak for supplying the materials. The materials used can be ordered by shopkeepers from: Kars & Co B.V., Ochten, the Netherlands • Avec B.V., Waalwijk, the Netherlands • Romak B.V., Hillegom, the Netherlands